PC

W9-ANG-066

36928

741.09   85-341
BLE

     Blegvad, Erik
     SELF-PORTRAIT

  Maumee Valley Country Day School
  Lower School Library

SELF-PORTRAIT: ERIK BLEGVAD

SELF-PORTRAIT:

ERIK BLEGVAD

written and illustrated by Erik Blegvad

with pictures also by
Harald Blegvad,
Julie Marstrand,
Albert Claudi Hansen,
Ib Andersen,
Agge Sikker Hansen,
& N. M. Bodecker

⚛ ADDISON-WESLEY

Text and illustrations Copyright © 1979 by Erik Blegvad
All Rights Reserved
Addison-Wesley Publishing Company, Inc.
Reading, Massachusetts 01867
Printed in the United States of America
ABCDEFGHIJK-WZ-79

Book designed by Charles Mikolaycak

Library of Congress Cataloging in Publication Data

Blegvad, Erik.
Self-portrait — Erik Blegvad.

SUMMARY: A well-known illustrator discourses on
himself, his life, and his work.
1. Blegvad, Erik. 2. Illustrators — United States —
Biography. [1. Blegvad, Erik. 2. Illustrators]
I. Title.
NC975.5.B55A2   1979   741'.092'4 [B] [92]   78-23765
ISBN 0-201-00498-4

Acknowledgements
These illustrations are reproduced through the
courtesy of the following:

pages 9, 11 (top)   *Les Pays Nordiques* by Doré
                      Ogrizek, Editions Odé, Paris, 1951
pages 10, 12   *Holiday,* Travel-Holiday, Floral
                      Park, New York (1969)
pages 13, 32   *Pepperidge Farm Cookbook* by
                      Margaret Rudkin, Atheneum
                      Publishers, New York City, 1963
pages 18, 19 (top)   *Elle,* Paris, 1950
pages 22, 23   *Mandens Blad*, Copenhagen, 1952
page 24   CBS/Woman's Day, New York
                      City, 1955
page 25   CBS/Woman's Day, New York
                      City, 1953

For

May 8th 1974

Lower School
Maumee Valley Country Day School

85-341

Rolig Dag paa Søen.

Skib i Kattegat
Marseylskuling.

6

My father, his father, and his father's
father all had drawing talent and all
hoped to become artists: none of them
did. My father became a marine biologist.
But he could always draw. He made
these two drawings when he was eight.
They were drawn in a physics class in
his father's school on the island of Samsö
in Denmark.

Father's older brother married an
artist, my Aunt Julie. She drew this
portrait of my father when he was a
young student in Copenhagen. It was in
Copenhagen that he later met and
married my mother and that's where my
sister Else and I were born. Else had
inherited a real talent and was the first
ever to show me how to draw.

Copenhagen in the twenties had less
than a million inhabitants. My own
favorite was "Bedstefar", my mother's
father.

Bedstefar was devoted to the king,
Christian the Tenth, who could trace
his royal family back a thousand years,
uninterrupted! Not many could do that.
As the three of us lived quite close
and we all enjoyed early morning
promenades, we met from time to time
— Grandfather and I, on foot, bowing
deeply — the king, I presume, saluting
from his horse. I bowed too deeply to
see the royal acknowledgment.

Grandfather made sure I saw
Copenhagen. We walked all over,
through parks, past palaces, into the
old and new harbors. He pointed out
the uniforms of soldiers, police and
postmen, often stopping to talk to
people. He was a retired schoolmaster
with an unusual gift for helping others
observe, listen, and learn. He read me
fairy and folk tales and told me stories
of his childhood herding cattle and
horses in the marshes on the west
coast of Jutland. He was old enough to
remember hiding the village horses
from the Austrians in the War of 1864.
Happily for me, he lived to be almost a
hundred.

Visages du Danemark

BEING A MAP
OF
DENMARK
(TO SIZE)

THE NORTH SEA

Jutland

Funen

Sealand

COPENHAGEN

THE BALTIC

(A SMALL MAP OF A SMALL COUNTRY)

9

Denmark in the thirties became my own fairyland. On my father's ship I sailed all its waters and visited all its harbors. In my school holidays I cycled all its roads. The one across Funen ends in Middelfart where my mother's sister was married to the local doctor. They had two children and a home where my sister and I were always welcome. There was always music in their home, for Aunt Edda was a pianist. Her brother, and my mother's, was an architect and often stayed there.

Uncle Albert had emigrated to the USA as a youth and had fought in the Great War with the U.S. Engineers. In the twenties he had returned to Denmark to recuperate from his war wounds: but in 1932 he died, still a young man. He drew this interior in the Middelfart folk museum.

Eneret. FOLKEMUSEET I MIDDELFART (Skorstensstuen)

Tegnet af Claudi Hansen.

We called her "Father's ship." It might as well have been, for although she belonged to the government's Marine Biological Station, he was in command. I sailed with him through the summers of the thirties. The ship was top heavy and most uncomfortable in a high sea. I became seasick for many years until on one voyage, miraculously, I found myself cured.

My father gave me a love of the sea, ships and boats, fish and oysters. It was against my instincts to kill a living animal, but my father, the expert, said, "Anything that tasty has only a rudimentary nervous system and feels no pain." I'm glad we had those years at sea together; he was rarely home.

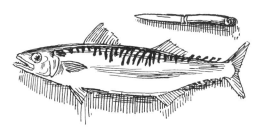

The compleat angler

My mother's devotion to art was absolute. Her eye was sure and nonconformist. Our home was full of paintings, drawings, and art books. My own attempts met only lavish praise and encouragement from her, and in 1941 during the German occupation of Denmark, I went to art school. There I met Niels Mogens Bodecker who became my lifelong friend.

The Germans had not stopped the publication of works by our best graphic artists. My favorites were Ib Andersen and Sikker Hansen. They drew for newspapers, made posters, and illustrated books.

In my graduation year I received my first assignment: a promotion piece for my father's book *Fishery in Denmark*. I drew the cover in Sikker's studio. He was a friend of the family and a kind and patient adviser. He himself was working on the original of this horseman in the summer landscape, only ten times bigger.

Ib Andersen gave me his sketch for *The Compleat Angler* (above) some years ago.

FISKERIET I DANMARK

The war ended. I had not seen my closest friend, Peter Steen, since 1939. He had become a pilot in the war and in the summer of 1946 he returned to Denmark just as my own military service ended. Before long he landed a job as flight instructor with a flying club outside Copenhagen. On weekends he flew stunts with a circus in the provinces, and he soon taught me to fly. That summer we were in love with aeroplanes, flying, and everything else in life. We "buzzed" Denmark from end to end. Beneath us lay all the landscapes I knew from the ships and bicycles of my childhood. Here we are over Kronborg Castle and the Elsinore shipyards with Sweden across the sound.

Later on, Peter became the editor of the newspaper where he and I first used to look for the drawings of Ib Andersen and Sikker Hansen. My friend from art school, Bodecker, and Peter also became friends.

There was always a party in Copenhagen in those heady years after the liberation, but Bodecker and I also had to earn a living. We made drawings for Peter's newspaper and for any one else who wanted them, sometimes in the middle of a party. This is one of Bodecker's drawings from June 1947.

KLODSMAJ
FINDER
EN SNAS

In July 1947 I went to Paris. I arrived with my bike, plenty of drawings, all my money, and ten pounds of butter. "As good as gold," my mother had said. Paris was hot and very foreign. It was also full of revellers celebrating the national holiday, Bastille Day. After dancing in the streets for two days and nights I was broke and the butter had melted. It was time to sell drawings. I went to the office of the magazine *Réalités*. They were preparing their annual *Salon d'Automobile* issue and miraculously asked me to do their cover. I had brought very few art materials with me and in my humble hotel room there was only a night table to work on, smaller than the drawing. I had one brush, some green poster paint, and a tube of white tempera. The cover was accepted and later on, on the newstands, I could spot its viridian glow from miles away.

Not until the following year did my fortunes really change. In the offices of the famous newspaper house *Paris Presse* an elegant lady looked at my drawings and in fluent English, my only international language, offered me as much work as I wanted for her weekly magazine *Elle*. She was Hélène Lazareff. Her husband, Pierre, also gave me work for his newspapers, *France Soir* and *France Dimanche*. Little by little, the French language lost some of its mystery. I was living in comfort in a city I had grown to love and had many exciting friends. Could there be more?

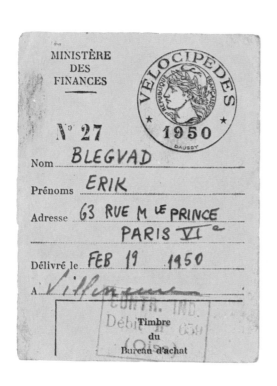

MINISTÈRE
DES
FINANCES

VELOCIPEDES
1950
DAUSSY

N° 27

Nom   BLEGVAD

Prénoms   ERIK

Adresse   63 RUE M LE PRINCE
PARIS VIe

Délivré le   FEB 19 1950

A   Villeneuve

Timbre
du
Bureau d'achat

CONTR. IND.
Débit N° 659

There was. I met Lenore Hochman from New York City. She was interested in everything that interested me, with the exception of flying. She was studying painting with Fernand Léger and André Lhote and lived on money sent from home. Lenore and I became inseparable. She introduced me to many of the ancient cities of Europe and to living with a cat. A black cat had already begun to appear in my drawings, but Lenore owned a live kitten! What's more, she fell in love with me as I had with her. One day on holiday in Austria we hitchhiked to Copenhagen and got married.

Here we are, back in Paris as man and wife. The drawings are pages from the sketch books I kept in those years.

We loved traveling, and one day we bought tickets to go to America.

20

Lower School
Maumee Valley Country Day School

85 - 341

In March 1951 we sailed for New York City. Here at last I met Lenore's family, her friends, and her home town. What a welcome! It even extended to the offices where I showed my drawings. "A nice art director is one who gives you a job," said an agent. I met many nice ones. My drawings subtly began to change. They became less decorative, less naive, more traditional and old fashioned. I drew at a feverish pace.

In August 1951 our son Peter was born. My ambition, which had never bothered me before, woke up and stretched. We bought a model A Ford!

Bodecker had also married an American and came to New York. Once more he and I were living and working in the same city.

In 1952 I was given an assignment which changed my life: the first set of illustrations for a children's book. I sensed that this was what I really wanted to do. I had never lost the visual imagination I had as a child. My earliest drawings had always been inspired by stories and tales.

In 1954 after a long visit to Europe, we moved to Westport, Connecticut. There our second son, Kristoffer, was born in June. Bodecker arrived, and this time we set up shop together. In our studio was a large bulletin board with a fine collection of misspellings of our two Danish names. That collection grew until 1966 when my family and I moved back to Europe, to live in London.

The *Woman's Day* calendar was originally created by Warren Chappel in the early fifties. Even then, the magazine had a reputation for above average art work. I certainly had to get above my own average to illustrate that famous calendar. But the more I drew the more obvious it became that some drawings simply were not as good as others. I've done twenty-four calendars, and I think these three drawings from 1955 are among my favorites.

When Mary Norton wrote *The Borrowers*, it immediately became a classic. It first appeared in America as a serial in *Woman's Day* and I did the illustrations. Here are three from Chapter One. I think they are still among my best children's book illustrations, although they were drawn for a magazine, not a book, many years ago.

Illustrating a children's book gives me a role which seems natural, accompanist rather than soloist. In a book, the pictures and words work together to tell a story. I also like the thought that books remain in homes longer than magazines. Eventually Lenore began to write children's books, and so we were able to work together as author and illustrator.

"I'LL TAKE THE CUP," HE SAID

'WELL, OUT OF MY WAY NOW,' SAID HOMILY

ERIK BLEGVAD

Preliminary sketches often have a freshness I tend to lose in the finished drawings. Below are two of a dozen attempts to find just the right title page for a book.

The rough on the facing page is from a book dummy and shows some of my second thoughts.

Had this been a chapter, I would have called it "Roughs, Revisions, Dummies, Doodles, and Decorated Envelopes." The next pages are for doodles.

HANS CHRISTIAN
ANDERSEN

THE SWINEHERD

Illustrated & Translated
by
Erik Blegvad

HARCOURT, BRACE & CO
1958

HANS CHRISTIAN
ANDERSEN

THE SWINEHER

Illustrated & Translated
by
Erik Blegvad

HARCOURT, BRACE &
1958

GIRL TOO BIG & NOT YOUNG ENOUGH   THE FINISHED DRAWING NARROWER

F. BLEGVAD.

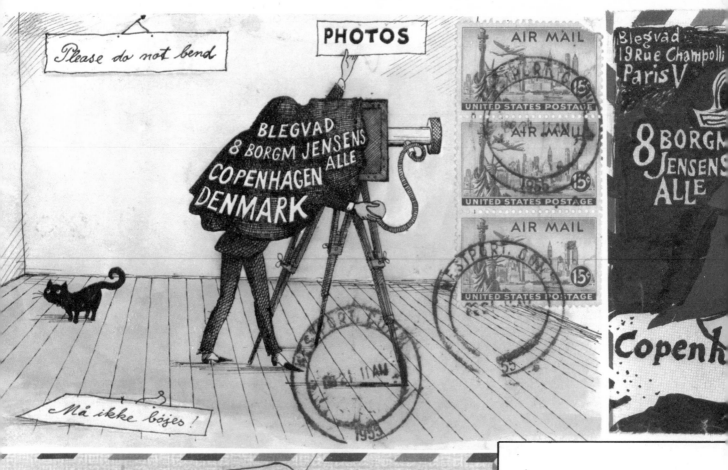

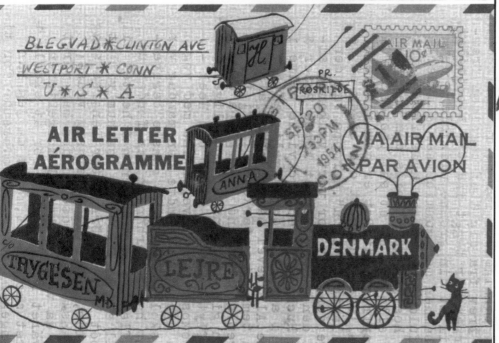

Decorated envelopes are for special people and special occasions. Peter Steen and I used them in our childhood, sometimes empty, just to test the postmen. These all had letters enclosed, and arrived safely without any complaints from my mother's patient postman.

There's a lazy side to me. I hold it
responsible for placing a sunrise north
of Copenhagen, or a sixth finger on
a decorated envelope, and for occasionally
making some stiff and graceless drawings.

But when my lucky side is working, I
find myself concentrated at the tip of my
pen, which to my delight, proceeds to
create people, objects, and worlds I
never knew existed.

To have learned to observe at such an
early age, to have stumbled into such a
varied life, to have spent it with such
extraordinary people — there's luck
for you.